The Importance of Nonprofit Board Leadership

A Guide to Creating a Highly Successful Nonprofit Board

Dennis C. Miller

BookLocker
Trenton, Georgia

Copyright © 2024 Dennis C. Miller

Paperback ISBN: 978-1-958891-38-4
Hardcover ISBN: 978-1-958891-39-1
Ebook ISBN: 979-8-88531-622-4

All rights reserved. No part of this publication may be reproduced, stored in a retrieval system, or transmitted in any form or by any means, electronic, mechanical, recording or otherwise, without the prior written permission of the author.

Published by BookLocker.com, Inc., Trenton, Georgia.

BookLocker.com, Inc.
2024

First Edition

Library of Congress Cataloguing in Publication Data
Miller, Dennis C.
The Importance of Nonprofit Board Leadership: A Guide to Creating a Highly Successful Nonprofit Board by Dennis C. Miller
Library of Congress Control Number: 2023924458

DISCLAIMER

This book details the author's four decades of personal experiences with and opinions about the importance of nonprofit board leadership. He is a nationally recognized expert in nonprofit board governance, but the author is not providing any legal advice. The author and publisher are providing this book and its contents on an "as is" basis and make no representations or warranties of any kind with respect to this book or its contents.

Except as specifically stated in this book, neither the author or publisher, nor any authors, contributors, or other representatives will be liable for damages arising out of or in connection with the use of this book. This is a comprehensive limitation of liability that applies to all damages of any kind, including (without limitation) compensatory; direct, indirect or consequential damages; loss of data, income or profit; loss of or damage to property and claims of third parties. You understand that this book is not intended as a substitute for consultation with a licensed attorney.

This book provides content related to the importance of nonprofit board leadership and the topics related to creating a highly successful nonprofit board. As such, use of this book implies your acceptance of this disclaimer.

Table of Contents

Introduction 1

Chapter 1: The Four Stages of Board Governance 5

Chapter 2: The Board & CEO Partnership 9

Chapter 3: The Required Competencies of Today's Nonprofit CEOs 13

Chapter 4: The Characteristics of Highly Successful Nonprofit Organizations 17

Chapter 5: The Role of the Board Chair 21

Chapter 6: Board Leadership Succession 25

Chapter 7: The Importance of Board Diversity 29

Chapter 8: Board Recruitment & Reappointment 33

Chapter 9: Board Committee Structures 39

Chapter 10: The Board's Role in Creating a Strategic Vision 45

Chapter 11: Building Your Positive Brand Identity 51

Chapter 12: Creating a Culture of Philanthropy 59

Chapter 13: Good Boards Evaluate the CEO; Great Boards Evaluate Themselves 67

Conclusion 71

Introduction

This book is about the importance of board leadership and how to create a highly successful nonprofit board. It is intended for the millions of people like you who volunteer their time as a member of a nonprofit organization board of trustees or directors, the CEOs who lead those organizations, and anyone who is inspired to serve their community as a nonprofit executive or board member in the future. Regardless of the mission of your organization or your role within it, you have made a commitment to have a positive impact on society locally, nationally, or globally.

My goal is to provide you with a proven roadmap to improve your board's performance. The recommendations in this book are based on decades of nonprofit board governance experience. When implemented, these strategies will help lead your organization toward greater effectiveness and impact. The benefits of serving as a board or executive leader of a highly successful nonprofit can be personal as well, for it is highly gratifying to know that you are bringing real value to the community.

Throughout the book, I will pose questions intended primarily for board discussion. I strongly suggest including at least one key question on every board meeting agenda, as a way to educate and engage your members on how to become a highly successful nonprofit board.

I believe it is important for everyone to be aware that nonprofit organizations are vital to our country's societal and economic well-being. They provide a wide range of services that are crucial to the public good including education, the arts, healthcare, social services, environmental protection, access to food and affordable housing, faith-based organizations, and more. Every nonprofit in its way provides the community with needed support, often transforming beliefs and hopes into action.

From the hospitals we were born in, the nursery schools and universities we attended, the youth organizations that helped us develop life skills, the museums and zoos we visited on family vacations, the theatrical performances we enjoyed, and the medical research that helped a loved one, we have experienced the impact of the nonprofit sector. These organizations are the glue that keeps our society together, especially during difficult times like our recent COVID-19 pandemic.

With 1.5 million nonprofit organizations in the United States employing 10% of the national workforce, the nonprofit sector is a significant economic driver. In fact, it is the third largest employer in the United States behind retail and manufacturing. The total annual revenue of the U.S. nonprofit sector is $2.6 trillion, comprising nearly 6% of our country's GDP.[1]

Nonprofit organizations vary significantly in size and scope, from small local charities to large international organizations. Seventy-six percent of nonprofits have annual revenues below $100,000 while 4% have annual revenues between $1M and $5M. The remaining 20% of our nonprofits have revenues above $5M while less than 0.2% have annual revenues of billions of dollars.[2]

Unfortunately, only around 50% of nonprofits are successful in our country. According to the National Center for Charitable Statistics, about

---

[1] "26 Incredible Nonprofit Statistics [2023]: How Many Nonprofits Are in the U.S.?" *Zippia*, 12 May 2023, www.zippia.com/advice/nonprofit-statistics/.
[2] Spirovski, Martin. "15 Interesting Nonprofit Organizations Statistics and Facts." *TeamStage*, 22 Sept. 2022, teamstage.io/nonprofit-organizations-statistics/.

30% of nonprofits will cease to exist in 10 years—and some experts predict the failure rate will be much higher.[3]

The truth is that is not enough to have a worthy cause or a passionate team. The biggest hurdle to success is executive leaders who lack the contemporary competencies and experience necessary to steer their organization toward success, and board members who have not had adequate training on nonprofit board governance and knowledge of what is required from them for their organization to be successful. Just because someone is a successful business executive, community leader, or prominent citizen in your community does not necessarily mean that they are prepared to become a good nonprofit board member. And even a nonprofit CEO who had success in the roles they held prior to becoming a chief executive can benefit from leadership education, coaching, and support to propel their board and leadership team forward.

With knowledge about what is needed to become a great nonprofit board and a deeper understanding of the nature of board leadership, every nonprofit can achieve a higher level of performance.

For almost four decades, I have had the privilege of working with wonderful people who have served as nonprofit CEOs, board members, and board chairs, many of whom have become close friends. I admire their personal commitment to their mission-driven organizations. But if we are going to truly increase the positive impact their organizations— and the entire sector – can have, we need to do all we can to ensure that everyone in the nonprofit community has knowledge about board

---

[3] "Get the Job You Really Want." *Zippia*, www.zippia.com/answers/what-percentage-of-nonprofits-are-successful/. Accessed 2 Oct. 2023.

governance best practices and an awareness of the competencies needed by today's nonprofit executive leaders.

As you work your way through this book, you will discover many opportunities to ask yourself whether or not your board is on the path to becoming highly successful. I hope you will consider using all that is offered in these pages to raise your organization's aspirations, and impact, to bring even greater value to those you serve.

Sincerely,

Dennis C. Miller
Founder & Chairman
DCM Associates, Inc.

Chapter 1:
The Four Stages of Board Governance

"The greatest leader is not necessarily the one who does the greatest things. He is the one that gets the people to do the greatest things."

Ronald Reagan

There is no more important topic to discuss about how to become a highly successful nonprofit board than to understand and learn about the four stages of nonprofit board governance. Becoming aware of what stage of governance your board is functioning at today will, more than anything else, help to put you on a more sustainable path to a successful future.

In their 2004 book, *Governance as Leadership: Reframing the Work on Nonprofit Boards*, authors Richard Chiat, Barbara Taylor, and William Ryan point out that the board of a newly created nonprofit organization will be very different than that of an organization that has been operating successfully for decades. They divide the evolution of a nonprofit's board into four stages in a way that resonates with my prior experience as a CEO and board chair.

They define the four stages of board governance as follows:

- Founding
- Fiduciary
- Strategic
- Leadership

A *founding* board does almost all the work of the organization, often without any paid staff. Their primary role is to get the organization off the ground. It is an exciting time, when a team of people who are passionate about a cause are working to bring a new organization to life.

The day-to-day level of volunteer energy required at the founding stage is not sustainable. Sooner or later, it will become difficult, if not impossible, to engage enough volunteer support to maintain operations. If an organization is to continue for the long term, the volunteers will need to hire paid staff to carry on the work. At this time, the board must transition to a *fiduciary* role, turning their focus to three primary legal responsibilities:

1. Duty of care, ensuring the prudent use of all assets, including facility, people, and goodwill.

2. Duty of loyalty, ensuring that the nonprofit's activities and transactions are, first and foremost, advancing its mission. The fiduciary board must be ready to recognize and disclose conflicts of interest and to make decisions that are in the best interest of the nonprofit corporation, rather than in the best interest of the individual board member (or any other individual or entity).

3. Duty of obedience, ensuring that the nonprofit obeys applicable laws and regulations, follows its own bylaws, and adheres to its stated corporate purposes/mission.

As the organization matures, in addition to the legal responsibilities, an effective board takes on a more strategic role and works with the CEO and executive leadership team to advise, develop, and monitor the implementation of a strategic plan and business plan.

The fourth stage of a board's developing role is one of *leadership*. Though the fiduciary and strategic roles remain important and continue as board functions, the ideal and mature role for any board desiring to succeed revolves around providing leadership to the organization in partnership with the chief executive officer. A leadership board accepts a sense of ownership, asking the right questions, putting forth new ideas and challenges, and partnering with the chief executive to continually refresh and renew the organization.

At the leadership stage it is important for the chief executive to feel a strong sense of security and self-confidence, to allow the board to be in partnership in leading the organization. For a nonprofit to succeed in fulfilling its mission and to have real impact in the community, it is imperative that the CEO and board grow together as partners.

Every stage of board development requires active commitment on the part of its members, but as the organization matures, the nature of the actions changes. The manner of board involvement in the founding stage will be very different from what is most beneficial at the leadership stage.

An effective board is aware of its point on the continuum of stages, understands its role and function within each stage, and participates accordingly. At no stage, however, can a nonprofit board afford to adopt the position of passive advisors.

Discussion Questions

- *At what stage or life cycle is our board functioning today?*
- *What challenges and opportunities exist today for our board and CEO to work more in partnership and leadership?*

- *In which stage of board governance might our organization generate greater results for our community?*

- *In which of the four stages would we feel most rewarded, and feel that our contributions were most beneficial?*

Chapter 2:
The Board & CEO Partnership

"Talent wins games, but teamwork and intelligence wins championships."

Michael Jordan

For any nonprofit to be successful, there must be a great partnership between the CEO and the board. Their ability to collaborate will ultimately determine the organization's effectiveness and success. The crucial qualities of this vitally important relationship are based on the following:

- A partnership built on trust
- A shared sense of accountability and responsibility
- Positive interaction that is focused on results
- Open and honest communication
- Mutual recognition and understanding that the chief executive works with the board but reports directly to the board chair

One of the characteristics of a highly successful nonprofit organization is the level of engagement between the board and the CEO. There needs to be a constant open and honest dialogue about the key issues the organization is facing and how to best utilize the talents, experience, and knowledge of each respective board member. It is also extremely important for every board member to feel that their voices are heard, that their actions matter, and that their ideas are encouraged for open discussion. It is the responsibility of both the board chair and CEO to make sure each board member is an engaged and active participant.

Unfortunately, one of the major complaints that I hear when I perform a board performance assessment is members' lack of engagement with the organization. One board chair told me that he was having a really difficult time engaging his board members. I decided to have a conversation with each member of his board. Four told me that if they missed their board meetings, they didn't feel like they had missed anything. I decided it was important for me to attend their next meeting.

The meeting was called to order and a motion to approve the minutes from the last meeting was approved. The CEO read word for word the report he had already emailed to all members of the board. The CFO provided a financial update, which she did extremely well. After a report from the facilities and program committees, the gala committee was asked to give an update on their plans to celebrate their 100th anniversary of the organization. After these reports, the board chair thanked everyone for attending and asked if anyone had any questions. They did not. As he adjourned the meeting, he reminded everyone that the next board meeting would be held in three months. Good night.

I now fully understood why those board members felt disconnected from the important work of this organization.

A great technique to encourage real engagement at board meetings is to practice what I call the 50% rule. In addition to the necessary reports and updates, add to the agenda a discussion question designed to bring the board's vision for the organization into focus. For example:

- What is the value we provide to the communities we serve?
- What is the image of our organization in our community?

- Why is our organization worthy of someone's gift?

Make sure that everyone at the meeting, board and executive team members alike, are invited and encouraged to answer the question. Not only will this promote vision alignment between the board and executive team, but it will also help to ensure that everyone at the meeting feels engaged and motivated. They are more likely to leave the meeting with confidence, enthusiastic about supporting the organization going forward. Now, this discussion might take up 20% to 80% of the meeting time, but in my experience, it takes about 50% of the meeting, which is why I call it the 50% rule.

Highly successful nonprofit organizations have strong executive and board leadership that believes the mission is best served when the organization is committed to continuous learning and improvement. With the self-confidence that comes from greater alignment, through ongoing dialogue between the board and executive leadership team, the entire organization's sense of teamwork will be enhanced and empowered.

Importantly, this elevates the experience of everyone involved in the organization, from volunteer board members to line staff. I mean, who doesn't enjoy working as a team to provide a positive impact in the community?

Discussion Questions

- *How would you describe the relationship your board has with the CEO?*

- *Would you describe it as a "partnership in leadership"?*

- *What do you feel the CEO and board need to do in order to create a stronger partnership?*

- *How might a CEO and board partnership benefit your organization and those you serve?*

Chapter 3:
The Required Competencies of Today's Nonprofit CEOs

"Before you are a leader, success is all about growing yourself. When you become a leader, success is all about growing others."

Jack Welch

The nonprofit sector has grown and changed dramatically over the last 50 years. Not only do nonprofits comprise a healthy segment of the national economy, the scope of their impact—and the professionalism required to ensure that impact—has expanded exponentially. With this, we have also seen a new set of ideal leadership competencies emerge. Here are the professional competencies that my executive search clients are most interested in seeing in candidates for chief executive (and other c-suite) roles:

- Visionary thinking. In the past the board set the future direction of the organization and asked the chief executive to implement the plan to achieve it. Today, boards are seeking CEOs who can step forward and lead the discussion on creating your strategic vision.

- Entrepreneurial spirit is perhaps the most significant new competency required by today's nonprofit boards. Nonprofit leaders today need to become the "chief entrepreneurial officer." Instead of just managing the organization's revenues, your CEO today needs to create new investments to allow for greater positive results, outcomes, and achievements.

- Emotional intelligence is the capacity to understand and manage your emotions. The skills involved in emotional intelligence are self-awareness, self-regulation, motivation, empathy, and social skills. People who are emotionally intelligent can identify what they are feeling; know how to interpret their emotions; understand how their emotions can impact others; can regulate their own emotions; and can manage other people's emotions.

- Relationships with internal and external stakeholders, including elected and appointed officials, business leaders, and key community leaders, is essential. Organizational leaders who can bring out the best in others, who can make people feel important and make people feel that their voices, concerns, and actions matter, will be far more successful than those who cannot.

- Collaboration is also essential, as we work to make our nonprofits successful in a time of limited resources and declining public sources of funding. High-performing boards encourage and reward their CEOs for seeking opportunities to collaborate with other, similarly mission-driven organizations. Many funders, in particular, do not appreciate the "silo mentality" of multiple organizations with similar missions operating in the same business market—and all asking for financial support. One prominent bank executive recently asked me, "Why aren't these organizations collaborating more?"

- Brand building helps prevent organizations from staying undercover as the "best-kept secret" in town. Today's nonprofit organizations must be achievement and results driven, and the

CEO needs to be out in front, effectively communicating to everyone the organization's success. The effective chief executive will make it a point to tell stories from the eyes of those the organization serves, and to illustrate the impact of its work in the community.

- Inspirational motivation describes a leader's ability to bring out the best in others. Successful leaders are able to make people feel important. They ensure that others' voices, concerns, and actions matter, and that their team members' individual goals are fully aligned with the organization's goals. Leaders who can do this will be very successful. They truly understand that leadership is an attitude, not a position.

Discussion Questions

- *How would you compare your CEO's competencies to the leadership competencies just described?*
- *How would you describe the relationship between your board and CEO?*
- *How does your CEO measure the success of your organization?*
- *How do you measure the success of your CEO?*

Chapter 4:
The Characteristics of Highly Successful Nonprofit Organizations

"Alone we can do so little; together we can do so much."

Helen Keller

Based on my experience, I have come to learn that there are 10 common characteristics of highly successful nonprofit organizations:

- Collaboration between the CEO and the board has resulted in an inspiring strategic vision that encourages commitment and provides real measures of success. According to Burt Nanus, an expert in visionary leadership, your vision should be "a realistic, credible, attractive future for your organization, a future that in important ways is better, more successful, or more desirable than your present."

- Board members feel a strong sense of ownership and partnership with the CEO and continually ask the right questions to continually refresh and renew the organization. Questions that a board member might ask include: "What is the value we provide to our community?" "What is our image in the community?" "How do we measure our success?"

- The CEO is a visionary thinker who has a high level of emotional intelligence and who has earned the trust and respect of their colleagues.

- The organization has established a positive and unique brand identity and communicates the achievements and positive results of the organization to internal and external stakeholders. Your organization can articulate what "distinguishes" your organization from others with similar missions.

- The executive leadership team demonstrates a strong sense of entrepreneurial spirit and seeks investors—not just funders—to generate new revenue streams. Successful nonprofit organizations transition from the tin cup theory of fundraising, asking *funders* for money based on the organization's needs, to the investment theory, where they seek *investors* to support their success.

- The organization continually seeks collaboration with similar mission-based organizations and does not always feel the need to "go it alone."

- The board has a recruitment plan that identifies gaps in board competencies, like leadership, strategic thinking, experience as a change agent, etc., and not just skill sets when seeking new members.

- The CEO, board, and chief development officer have created a positive culture of philanthropy where everyone works together to cultivate and solicit donors who are eager to invest in the success of the organization and the needs of those it serves.

- Board members regularly assess the organization's performance and continually identify potential improvements to further sustain the mission.

- The organization recognizes and rewards the contributions of high-performing staff, board, volunteers, and donors to celebrate the hard work of everyone involved.

Highly successful nonprofit organizations experience increased demand for their services, high morale among staff and board, and increased donors and dollars, and have a greater positive impact on those they serve. However, there are also a number of common obstacles to becoming a highly successful nonprofit board:

- Failure to engage and communicate effectively among board members
- Failure to effectively recruit new members
- Lack of clear criteria for reappointment of board members to new terms
- Inability to select a board chair
- Having an "inner and outer" board (usually resulting in too many executive committee meetings)
- Inability to honestly address the poor performance of board members or the CEO
- Inability to overcome fears and insecurities of board members related to fundraising
- Nonalignment of the organization's vision and goals with committee structures

Highly successful nonprofit boards constantly reexamine themselves and commit to improving their work. It takes courage for the board to take a look at itself. Isn't this what the board would expect from their CEO?

In previous chapters we discussed board engagement and communication. In the sections ahead, I will help you learn how to overcome all of the remaining obstacles as well.

Discussion Questions

- *What characteristics of highly successful nonprofits does your organization possess?*
- *What specific aspects of your board's governance would you like to improve?*
- *What are the obstacles your board is struggling with today?*
- *What solutions to the obstacles have you tried?*

Chapter 5:
The Role of the Board Chair

"If your actions inspire others to dream more, learn more, do more and become more, you are a leader."

John Quincy Adams

The role and responsibilities of the nonprofit board chair include leading the board and serving as the direct supervisor of the CEO who runs the daily operations of the organization. The board chair position requires an exceptional commitment to the organization, first-rate leadership qualities, and personal integrity. The board chair must also have earned the respect of fellow board members by demonstrating that they are able to meet the challenges of the position. The board chair needs to be an inspirational leader.

The board chair helps the board as a whole to think strategically about the organization's achievements for mission, vision, and long-term goals, in the context in which it operates. The board chair must be a strong strategic thinker who is able to make difficult decisions and who is willing to be accountable for the organization's sustainability.

While the board chair is the chief volunteer officer and is charged with leading the board, the entire weight of the board's work cannot fall on the shoulders of one person. The board chair delegates to and empowers board members, encouraging each of them to take ownership of their assigned responsibilities.

The board chair, in partnership with the CEO, steers the nonprofit organization toward achieving its vision and strategic goals. This includes the following required actions:

- Working behind the scenes to build consensus among members of the board
- Helping the entire board think strategically about mission and vision
- Leading the entire board in making sure all board work is accomplished
- Supervising and building a strong and supportive relationship with the CEO
- Appointing members of the board to serve as committee chairs
- Facilitating board meetings and approving meeting agendas
- Ensuring that all board members are engaged and participating in all board decisions
- Communicating with all board members on a regular basis
- Staying abreast of the board governance committee's recommendations and decisions regarding board recruitment and reappointment
- Serving as an ex-officio member of all board committees
- Leading the board's evaluation of the CEO on an annual basis
- Ensuring that the board's performance is measured on a regular basis too

Consider also the characteristics of a high-performing leader. In my experience, the most effective, impactful board chairs are:

- Trusted and respected colleagues

- Effective decision-makers with excellent judgment
- Experienced leaders who to lead with integrity
- Experienced board members
- Excellent communicators
- Committed to the significant time requirements of the board chair role
- Politically savvy

Discussion Questions

- *As a board chair, how would you compare your role and responsibilities to these best practices?*
- *As a board chair, what are your greatest challenges when it comes to leading your board?*
- *What are your greatest achievements this year as board chair?*
- *Have you started to consider board leadership succession planning?*

Chapter 6:
Board Leadership Succession

"A leader's lasting value is measured by succession."

John C. Maxwell

Board leadership succession is an ongoing process and responsibility of the board. I often tell boards that the best date to begin searching for the next board chair is the first day of the newly appointed chair's term.

Unfortunately, many organizations struggle in their efforts to identify, recruit, and select a chair. I have compiled a list of the obstacles that I most frequently see in my work with nonprofit organizations:

- Perception that the job requires too much time and too much work.
- Lack of preparedness or board training for potential candidates.
- Too much board politics or bureaucracy.
- Very few rewards and recognitions for those who serve as chair.
- The board structure and committees are not properly structured, and board roles are poorly defined.
- The current board chair has not planned and groomed a successor.
- The current board chair cannot relinquish control of the reins.
- No one on the board ever discusses the issue during the term of the current board chair.

- The leadership potential of new board candidates is never considered.

The first step in recruiting a board chair is to immediately begin an assessment of the leadership potential of current board members. It is crucial to continually consider who on your board is high performing and who demonstrates the skills and capabilities needed to succeed in a leadership role.

Here are additional, concrete action steps that will continue leading you in the right direction:

- Ask your current board chair to identify potential candidates from the current board.

- Begin a series of discussions with potential candidates regarding their interest in assuming the role.

- Identify the specific type of training or coaching these candidates might want to help them prepare for greater board responsibility.

- Unless absolutely necessary, it is preferable to identify your new board chair from current members.

- Institute ongoing training for all current board members in all aspects of board governance.

- Consider offering the chair-elect a professional board coach/mentor to support their transition during their first term in office.

- Find ways to reward and recognize those who serve on your board.

- Provide opportunities for all board members to participate in a wide array of committees, task forces, and advisory boards.
- Build a culture of success that strives for excellence in all you do to create a winning attitude.
- Recognize former board chairs either through a formal recognition program or an annual benefit event.
- Make the role of being the board chair something special.

Discussion Questions

- *How does your board address leadership succession?*
- *Does your board provide ongoing governance training?*
- *How do you reward and recognize board leadership?*
- *What difficulties, if any, is your organization having identifying a new chair?*

Chapter 7:
The Importance of Board Diversity

"In diversity there is beauty and there is strength."

Maya Angelou

Today, most people when discussing diversity on their board are referring to the representation of individuals from a wide variety of backgrounds, including but not limited to gender, race, age, sexual orientation, and disabilities. Many use the term "Diversity, equity, and inclusion (DEI)" in their efforts to ensure that all voices are heard and that different perspectives are considered in decision-making processes. My colleagues and I also like to add "belonging" (DEI&B). Others, when discussing diversity on the board, are referring to the need for individuals with different cognitive styles, experiences, problem-solving approaches, skills, and competencies.

When people from different backgrounds and experiences are on the board, it can lead to better decision-making, more creativity, and a better reputation. I think both concepts of diversity are important but, today, more than ever before, having your board comprised of individuals who most reflect the composition of those you serve is crucial to becoming a successful board.

The benefits of diversity also make for more effective board meetings. Having an opportunity to hear different perspectives on a topic makes for much better decision-making. Decisions and subsequent recommendations will be well-rounded and comprehensive. By drawing on the varied experiences of each board member, decisions can be made with a fuller understanding of their potential implications.

From my experience, a diverse group of people with varying ideas can also help foster and drive creativity and innovation. It's beneficial for board members with different backgrounds, who may have experienced things differently, to come together and brainstorm new solutions and initiatives that would benefit the organization and ultimately those the organization serves. Oftentimes, new possibilities open up what might never have been considered before. Studies have shown that organizations with diverse boards tend to perform better than those that don't.

It has also been my experience that boards that reflect the diversity of those being served in their community have enhanced reputations. It certainly builds trust and respect and allows people to be more comfortable engaging with you as opposed to sending out a mission and values statement, which is nothing more than words. A commitment to diversity builds strong relationships and trust.

Achieving diversity on your board can be difficult at first. There may be unconscious bias on the part of some board members. However, boards today should invest time and effort to create a recruitment process to identify candidates who possess both the qualifications and experiences and bring a wide variety of backgrounds onto the board. Creating a diverse board may also help you recruit better board members who want to be part of an organization committed to diversity.

Embracing diversity, equity, inclusion, and belonging on your board and creating a diverse team of many talents and experiences will result in an organization that generates successful outcomes for those it serves.

Discussion Questions

- *Has your board provided any training on the importance of diversity?*
- *How does your board define diversity?*
- *Has your board discussed how best to recruit diverse candidates?*
- *How successful has your board been in recruiting candidates from diverse backgrounds?*

Chapter 8:
Board Recruitment & Reappointment

"Great vision without great people is irrelevant."

Jim Collins, author

A board that commits to a thoughtful recruiting process will build and sustain a board that is noted for its vitality. But what exactly constitutes the most effective way to identify the right board members for your organization?

Most boards identify and recruit new members by asking people they know if they would like to serve on their nonprofit organization's board. Many excellent board members are recruited this way, but as a board-building strategy it is limited. Recruiting board members without first reflecting on the qualities and characteristics that are most needed by your organization will cause your board to continue to struggle.

I have developed a simple five-step methodology to recruit the board members you really need, not just those you know.

Step 1

Develop an ideal board matrix to describe the personal characteristics and attributes of the "ideal board" for your organization. These personal characteristics may include, but not be limited to, the following:

- Inspirational leadership
- Influence
- Brand builder

- Change agent
- Influencer
- Innovative/strategic thinking
- Decision-maker
- Collaborator

Remember that personal characteristics or attributes are *not skills*—like certified public accountant, doctor, lawyer, professor, social worker, etc. Skills are important to bring to a board, but consideration of them comes later in the process.

Step 2

Develop a current board matrix mapping the personal characteristics and attributes of the current board.

Step 3

Compare the ideal board matrix created in Step 1 and the current board matrix created in Step 2 and look for the gaps. What key characteristics or attributes are lacking in your current board? Which ones are priorities for the organization? Based on your identification of the most desired personal characteristics and attributes, engage your board and stakeholders in identifying individuals who possess such characteristics and attributes.

During this stage, you should be contacting key business, community, and civic leaders, asking them who they think might be a good board member who meets your competency priorities. Reach beyond your "inner circle" of contacts.

For example, if being a strategic thinker was a missing competency on your board, you can begin by asking the leaders you know, "Who do you consider to be a good strategic thinker in our community?" Get others involved in your work to identify people with certain competencies to join your board.

Step 4

After you rank the potential candidates according to your specific characteristic needs—such as innovative thinker, change agent, etc.—then, and only then, begin to rank them according to your need for specific skills.

Going back to the need for a strategic thinker for your board, consider how you might handle finding two excellent candidates who possess that competency. One is a CPA and the other is a business executive. At that point, you can consider which skill might be more beneficial to the board. Also, diversity is crucial as well. Which candidates help your board become more reflective of the community you serve, as we just discussed previously?

Recruiting individuals who have specific skills will bring important resources to your board. But identifying—and then addressing—key gaps in the personal characteristics in the composition of your board will raise it to a higher level of performance.

Step 5

Invite highly ranked candidates for an interview with select board members to discuss their potential interest in serving on the board.

Nominating individuals who are known to your current board members is one appropriate strategy for board-building, but it should not be your *only* strategy. The ideal board consists of individuals who are recruited based on agreed-upon criteria that first considers personal characteristics or attributes and *then* considers professional skills.

Once you begin to recruit board members based on ideal characteristics first and skills second, you will be on your way to building a high-performing nonprofit board that is ready and able to have a profound impact in the community.

One of the other major responsibilities of the board is to ensure that a process is in place to evaluate an individual board member's performance prior to rewarding that member with a new term. The board must continually evaluate each member's performance and make the difficult decision not to reappoint when it is appropriate and in the best interest of the board.

This process really begins during the recruitment and orientation process, by explaining the expectations of each new member. It continues during each year through the board's educational activities and annual goal-setting procedures. The expectations of each board member and the board as a whole should be an ongoing conversation. It should never be a surprise when the governance committee decides not to reappoint someone to the board.

If your board does not have a reappointment process, which includes a fact-based evaluation of individual performance against expectations, it should be developed. Key aspects of this process are:

- Preparing a written job description for board members.
- Keeping attendance records for board and committee meetings.

- Developing a target profile for representation (e.g., functions, professions, diversity, etc.) that you want for the board.
- Creating an annual checklist to evaluate the contributions of board members whose terms will expire.
- Developing a self-evaluation tool for board members whose terms are expiring.

Discussion Questions

- *How does your board currently go about recruiting new members?*
- *What would be the ideal characteristics of a board member?*
- *From your perspective, what is most important in recruiting new members?*
- *Do you ask board members whose terms are up for renewal to complete a self-assessment of their performance?*

Chapter 9:
Board Committee Structures

"The achievements of an organization are the results of the combined efforts of each individual."

Vince Lombardi

Based on my experience, the best board committee structure is one that is kept as simple as possible. Committees are developed to help the board do the work that is required. The fewer the standing committees, the better. Each committee needs a chair that is appointed by the board chair. The board chair should inform the board of their committee chair appointments. Though the entire board does not need to approve the chair's selections, it is important for the board to know who the committee chairs will be for the upcoming year. Goals for each committee need to be established that reflect the overall goals of the organization.

The chair of the committee, in consultation with the board chair, should determine the composition of the committee and invite those interested to serve. Each board member should serve on at least one committee.

Each committee should be evaluated annually to determine if it is achieving its goals, contributing to the overall success of the board, and is appropriately sized and populated. It is highly desirable to have board and non-board members on each committee. Appointing non-board members to serve on committees creates an excellent "farm system" for new board members.

Committees should not meet just to meet. If there are no important action items on your board or committee agenda, consider canceling the meeting. Having them attend unnecessary meetings is counterproductive.

I do think there are a few important committees that every board should have. They are as follows:

Executive Committee: There are only two purposes of the executive committee.

> 1) To meet during an emergency when it would be difficult to convene the full board to meet. This is often the case when a board resolution must be approved for banking issues or grant funding applications. The executive committee is the only committee that has the power and authority to make decisions for the board.

> 2) The executive committee can also be a "sounding board" for the chief executive who wishes to discuss key issues prior to presenting them to the full board.

However, too often executive committees are scheduled inappropriately, creating the impression that there is "an inner board and an outer board," especially to those not on the executive committee. You do not want your board to feel that all board decisions are made by the executive committee and your role is just to approve of their decisions.

Depending on how often the full board meets, the executive committee can meet during the months when the full board is not meeting.

Governance Committee: The governance committee, in my opinion, is the most important committee of the board. Traditionally, nonprofit boards had nominating committees to recruit and recommend new board members. The term "nominating committee" implies a primary responsibility for recruiting new members. Over time, boards also realized that educating new and current members on a wide array of topics was also important throughout the terms of the members. Discovering that everyone benefits from education, not just new members, this committee's name evolved into the "board development committee." However, that name often became confused with the development committee charged with fundraising. Thus, the newly adopted term for board recruitment and development is the governance committee.

The governance committee has the following key responsibilities:

- Periodically review and update the roles and responsibilities of the board (as a whole) as well as individual board members.

- Assess the current and future board composition requirements and develop a profile of the board as it should evolve over time.

- Identify potential new board members.

- Nominate new individuals and reappoint current members, which we described previously.

- Assess board effectiveness on an annual basis.

- Periodically review and update board practices and policies.

- Ensure board and chief executive succession planning.

- Nominate board members for election as board officers.

- Plan and schedule board retreats.

- Provide ongoing education to all board members on important governance issues.

Strategic Development Committee: This is an important committee that can meet quarterly or every two months to review the status of the implementation of your strategic plan, marketing and communications strategies, discussion of affiliations and/or mergers, progress being made toward achieving your vision, and adherence to your values.

Other key committees of the board often include finance, audit, human resources and compensation, fundraising and development, and investments. Effective board meetings require prior planning with the board chair, and chief executive especially, to decide on the key question for ensuring the engagement and motivation of the board. They should discuss the key action items that will be required for approval, any anticipated obstacles, and the amount of time being allotted for each item when preparing the meeting agenda. It is very important for the board chair to keep the meeting moving and prevent "too much stray" from the agenda. No one wants to attend unproductive meetings that are run unnecessarily.

I would also like to mention briefly the appropriate use of advisory boards and task forces. Advisory boards can be a very effective tool when utilized appropriately, and when misused they can be a public relations disaster. Many organizations create advisory boards to solicit advice on a specific issue and wish to gather individuals from the community who may have the expertise needed. The key to an advisory board's success is simple: Make sure that the members understand their purpose, give them specific responsibilities, and listen to their advice.

If you are going to ask someone for their "advice," make sure you "act" upon it when given. Too many advisory boards are created to "find a place" for older board members or because it looks like a great idea at the time. The enthusiasm of those invited to serve on the advisory board often dissipates quickly, and the gap between expectation and performance is enormous.

A task force is different from an advisory board in that it is established for a specific objective, such as planning a retreat or reviewing bylaws, within a specific period of time. Upon completion of the work, the group disbands.

Discussion Questions

- *Is the majority of time at your board meetings spent on reporting the past or discussing the future?*
- *Does your board evaluate each committee's purpose and goals on an annual basis?*
- *Do you solicit and invite "non-board members" to serve on a committee both for their expertise and for "grooming" them to potentially serve on the board?*
- *Does your executive committee create the perception of "an inner and outer board"?*

Chapter 10:
The Board's Role in Creating a Strategic Vision

"Greatness is not where we stand, but in what direction we are moving."

Oliver Wendell Holmes

In my book *The Power of Strategic Alignment: A Guide to Energizing Leadership and Maximizing Potential in Today's Nonprofit Organizations*, I identified the key steps necessary to go beyond the traditional strategic planning process to achieve long-term success and sustainability. This innovative concept that I developed is called *Strategic Alignment*, which refers to the process of aligning all stakeholders, both internally and externally, to be focused and committed to achieving one goal: the organization's vision. In addition, the concept requires the development of new competencies and non-traditional skill sets for both executive and board leadership.

The traditional way most nonprofit organizations embark on their strategic planning process often begins with high hopes but concludes in disappointment with little achieved and the report often ending up sitting on some executive's shelf collecting dust. This disappointment is commonly the result of most strategic plans lacking the following four components:

- An upfront, comprehensive assessment of the organization to identify key strengths and crucial areas of needed improvement.
- A clear vision with established measures of successful progress to align the entire organization's efforts.

- A comprehensive funding plan to secure the necessary resources.

- And a detailed plan for implementation and execution with buy-in from both the board and staff.

Sometimes in life the simplest things can be the most difficult. This is often the case with creating your organization's vision. Mostly everyone knows that mission answers the question "What is your purpose?" and that vision answers "Where are you going?" I really don't know why, but just asking the simple question "What is your vision?" can be the biggest strategic challenge most organizations have to confront.

Perhaps because we are all mired in our day-to-day struggles with our long-term planning horizon not going beyond next week, most of us have difficulty answering this question. Oftentimes, they answer by citing their purpose or "We just want to survive." Though often a true statement, it will not inspire your key stakeholders to be motivated going forward.

Yet in spite of the challenge, one must answer this question before any effective strategic plan can proceed. This is important because it sets the stage for leadership to chart a new direction or future view of the organization. As a former CEO and board chair, I know firsthand the daily difficulties and challenges everyone faces in managing the day-to-day operations of our organizations. Still, a leader needs to articulate the vision and build a strategic plan to make the vision become a reality.

In days gone by, the board set the vision and management was told to implement the plan to achieve it. Today, an effective leader must work in partnership with the board to create the organization's future direction. They don't wait for their boards to create the vision; they must have the courage to develop and communicate their hopes for the future. It takes courage to set the vision. The board needs to work in partnership with the CEO in creating the vision that meets the definition below from Bart Nanus.

According to Nanus, author of *Visionary Leadership* and several other books on leadership, vision is a realistic, credible, attractive future for your organization. Your vision is your articulation of a destination toward which your organization should aim, a future that in many important ways is better, more successful, or more desirable than your present. It is a signpost pointing the way for all who need to understand what the organization is and where it intends to go. Nanus goes on to state, "Successful leaders know that nothing drives an organization like an attractive, worthwhile, achievable vision for the future."

Based on my experience, your vision should set standards of excellence, inspire enthusiasm, encourage commitment, and be well articulated and easily understood. Above all, your vision should be ambitious.

Now that the board and CEO have agreed upon the vision for your organization, the board must ensure the leadership team has developed the right strategies to accomplish it and knows what specific actions have to be taken and by whom and when.

The board's role in the strategic planning process is simple:

- It all starts with your vision statement. Make sure you can measure your progress toward achieving it. If you cannot measure the progress toward achieving it, go back and start over.

- Have the executive leadership team provide an update on the progress of achieving goals at least on a quarterly basis.

- Stay focused on the crucial issues. I have seen too much time and energy wasted by spending an inordinate amount of time on issues and information that are not critical to building the organization's future success.

- Keep the process simple. Don't make it any more complex than necessary.

- Make sure you seek good ideas from everyone. Listen to your stakeholders' different points of view. Encourage people to speak candidly about their hopes for the organization and what they would like to see accomplished. It is amazing to learn how many organizations never consider asking their key donors to participate in their strategic planning process yet get disappointed when they don't contribute to their expected potential.

- Build a plan that is connected to people's heartfelt emotions. If people are not passionate about the plan, they will most likely not participate in its implementation at the level required for success.

- Invest the required time to develop an implementation plan. The biggest reason for failure is not properly investing the time and resources for execution.

- Know who will be responsible for what specific action and know what the timelines are.

- Focus on results and deal decisively with all obstacles your organization faces in producing the desired outcomes. While the perceived obstacle to success is external, the reality is that more organizations fail because they cannot resolve their internal conflicts.

- Be prepared to modify your implementation plan based on new information that becomes available.

- Communicate your plan to all key stakeholders. It is amazing how many people have told me, "They asked for my input, but then never got back to me on the final results of the plan." It is more and more important today to promote your achievements and successful results. If you don't tell them, who will?

- Make sure you have developed a list of success factors for measuring and monitoring your progress. Creating a one-page Scorecard for your board members and leadership team is a great way for everyone to focus on the important issues. Place a green dot on those strategies where progress is being achieved, a yellow dot where the outcome is less certain but still a work in progress, and a red dot when nothing is currently being achieved. In order to spend your time wisely, focus on red dots first and then yellow dots second. Spending all of your time patting yourselves on the back because of those green dots may leave the others unaddressed and results hard to come by.

I always advise my clients to focus on a few important goals. Whenever an organization tells me they are working on 10 different goals, I always know that their chance of actually achieving anything goes down dramatically. Have you ever really achieved anything when you have more than four goals at a time? For most of you, the honest answer is no. Another bit of good advice is to make sure that your goals have the following characteristics:

- Specific: They must be clear and easily understood.

- Measurable: If you cannot measure your goals, how will you know if you are ever really achieving them?

- Attainable: They must be realistic, yet a bit of a stretch to achieve.

- Relevant: They must be an important tool in reaching your organization's vision.

- Timetables: They must have beginning and ending points.

Discussion Questions

- *Is your current strategic vision stale and in need of revitalization?*

- *Are you still passionate about achieving it?*

- *Is your new vision a realistic, credible, attractive future for your organization?*

- *Will your new vision inspire your staff, board, and donors to achieve it?*

Chapter 11:
Building Your Positive Brand Identity

"Your brand is the single most important investment you can make in your business."

Steve Forbes

The concept of developing brand identity is a cornerstone of all for-profit business strategies yet is fairly new for the nonprofit sector. Many nonprofits continue to use their brands primarily as a fundraising tool, but a growing number are moving beyond that approach to explore the wider, strategic roles that brands can play driving broad, long-term social goals, while strengthening internal identity, cohesion, and capacity. According to a study at Harvard University supported by the Rockefeller Foundation, branding is a matter for the entire nonprofit executive team and the board. At every step in an organization's strategy and at each juncture in its theory of change, a strong brand is increasingly seen as critical in helping to build operational capacity, galvanize support, and maintain focus on the social mission.

Brand identity is the total promise that your organization makes to your clients, employees, board, donors, and volunteers. Brand identity is the aggregation of all your organization does—its mission, vision, personality, and promise to those you serve. It is a means of identifying and distinguishing your organization from others. An organization with a unique brand identity has improved brand awareness, a motivated team of employees who feel proud working for a well-branded organization, and active board members and donors. Brand identity leads to brand loyalty, brand preference, and high credibility. It assures the customers again and again that you are who you say you are. It establishes an immediate connection between the organization and consumers. Brand identity should be sustainable. It is crucial so that the consumers instantly correlate with your programs and services.

Your organization should develop the following areas to build a positive identity:

- Review your current core values and make sure that you are actually living them every day. It's one thing to have your values listed on your website and brochure; it is another to make sure they are a reality.

- Review your client satisfaction surveys to understand how they feel about your services and programs and then make the necessary adjustments.

- Revise and update your website with new content along with video testimonials from those you serve. Having clients speak about the positive impact your organization has had on themselves or their families is very powerful.

- Review all of your communication and public relations messages to ensure that they articulate who you are and how you are distinguished from others.

- Ensure that all individual and organizational achievements, positive outcomes, results, and awards are prominently displayed in your facilities, on your website, and in public relations communications.

- Discuss your achievements, positive outcomes, results, and awards with your employees, board, volunteers, donors, and all stakeholders at every opportunity to build strong internal relationships and community ambassadors.

- Understand why donors contribute to you and what benefit you have provided them.

- Develop a speakers bureau for the community to enable professionals and leadership to present relevant information, building strong community relationships.

Encouraging your CEO to become a "thought leader" in your community is a terrific strategy to help brand your organization. Being a thought leader is becoming a core business strategy for a burgeoning number of professionals, firms, and associations. It's difficult to find an exact definition that is universally accepted, but a thought leader is someone who is known for their innovative ideas and expertise and is widely recognized as a source of guidance in their industry. One of the recurring themes many clients complain about is the lack of community awareness and knowledge of who they are. Too often I hear "We are the best kept secret in town" and I say: Why is that?

Your organization should organize and coordinate a series of meetings and conferences with community, civic, government, education, and business leaders on a range of topics that impact the lives of those in the community. For example, one behavioral health client invited local ministers, police chiefs, court officials, school superintendents, etc., to a series of meetings dealing with "at-risk youth." The purpose of these meetings was as follows:

- Demonstrate their expertise on the topic.

- Provide an opportunity to build a reputation as a leading community advocate.

- Build new relationships with key leaders in the community.
- Enhance ability to receive grant funding through collaboration.
- Coordinate a regional community plan of action.
- Generate positive public relations and visibility.

Identifying trends at an early stage or creating ideas that change the future for the community are characteristics of being a thought leader. Another of the positive results of being a thought leader is to increase your organization's name recognition in the community. You could develop better outreach to the community, new programs, or enhanced existing programs based on emerging community needs and funding identified by those willing to invest in successful patient outcomes.

Every successful nonprofit organization is a brand. When we think of the American Red Cross, the Make-A-Wish Foundation of America, or the Bill & Melinda Gates Foundation, what comes to your mind is a very well-branded nonprofit organization. These are iconic nonprofits whose very name conjures up a host of associations, memories, and positive feelings. Branding is not just marketing and advertising (though they are key activities promoting your brand). Larry Checco, nonprofit consultant and author of *Branding for Success: A Roadmap for Raising the Visibility and Value of Your Nonprofit Organization*, says that every organization can use branding to create visibility and convince supporters of the organization's value.

One suggestion for you to consider is to develop a few focus groups for your organization from people in your community. Keep the groups small (more than eight but less than 20) to better manage the discussion. Ask them open-ended questions about the following:

- When you hear our name, what feelings and thoughts come to mind?
- What is our reputation in the community?
- Do we properly communicate our values?
- Do we demonstrate our commitment to client service?
- What does our brand represent?

With all the focus today on social media and mobile technology, we often forget how important a role your website plays in branding your organization. You don't need to spend a fortune to have a decent website, but it should be kept up to date. If your home page is still showing a picture of your gala from three years ago, it's a good time to make changes.

A monthly or quarterly newsletter highlighting any recent achievement or success is another key component of your branding strategy. It should keep your stakeholders updated with possible links back to your website. I highly recommend to many organizations that are just starting a newsletter to consider utilizing Constant Contact, an inexpensive online tool for creating newsletters, social media marketing, and online surveys. Constant Contact, Inc. wrote the book on Engagement Marketing™—the new marketing success formula that helps small organizations create and grow customer relationships in today's socially connected world. Through its unique combination of online marketing tools and free personalized coaching, Constant Contact helps small businesses, associations, and nonprofits connect and engage with their next great customer, client, or member. Launched in 1998, Constant Contact has long championed the needs of small organizations, providing them with an easy and affordable way to create and build successful, lasting customer relationships.

Another key recommendation for creating your brand on your website is through the use of a web-based video. The best people to tell your story are often the ones who receive services from you. It is relatively easy to produce a three- to five-minute video for your website that will appeal to both their minds and hearts. This video may begin with the executive director or board chair providing a warm welcome, followed by testimonials and photos of those served by your organization. You may also want to have a key donor or two included in the video to explain why they support your organization. It is amazing what powerful, heartfelt stories your clients can tell.

One final thought on branding. I think it is very effective for nonprofit organizations to let people know who serves on your board as well as their professional background and expertise. Of course, no personal information or contact information should be displayed, but I think your board reflects who you are and I think they should be prominently displayed under "About Us." I also think the leadership team with photos, titles, and contact information should be readily available.

Discussion Questions

- *How is your organization different from others? What makes it unique?*

- *Can members of your board easily articulate the top achievements of your organization this past year?*

The Importance of Nonprofit Board Leadership

- *How do you let everyone in your community know the positive impact you are having on people's lives?*

- *Do you have a branding strategy today?*

Chapter 12:
Creating a Culture of Philanthropy

"It's not how much we give but how much love we put into giving."

Mother Teresa

Let me know if the following statement describes your organization:

Board members would rather "stick pins" in their eyes than have anything to do with raising money.

The mere mention of the word "fundraising" creates anxiety and discomfort. Why is this? There are a number of reasons, but the biggest is the fear of rejection. Another reason is "If I ask them for money, they may ask me for money." Is this true for your board?

Another problem for many organizations is that they view the Development Office as a department—like finance, human resources, or quality improvement. The development efforts are disconnected from the work of the organization. Boards do not see the connection between the organization's success and the success of their fundraising efforts. Development needs to be an attitude integrated into all aspects of the organization, not just a department down the hall. I will shortly describe what I call the "fundraising Bermuda Triangle" and how to avoid it. And too many organizations ask for money because of their financial distress than their organizational success—a term I coined the "tin cup theory of fundraising."

How many of you have experienced the following?

Your board development committee meets and the chairperson calls the meeting to order. They review the fundraising plan for the upcoming year: *There is talk about the gala—who can we honor and where should it be held? Where is this year's golf outing and who will agree to chair it? How about the wine tasting—how much can we raise?*

The committee reviews the standard list of donor prospects that were assigned to each committee member and the chair says, "Did anyone call their list of prospects? A long silence and then, "Okay, let's move on to discuss the table settings for the gala. Let's put this on next month's agenda; hopefully more people will attend the meeting." Little has been accomplished or achieved.

The overwhelming number of people who serve on your boards are well-meaning people. They want to do the right thing. They want your organization to succeed. But why doesn't it happen? Why does everything that deals with fundraising feel like pulling teeth?

Let's start our discussion with an understanding of why people really give money—the Principles of Philanthropy.

- They give because they want to.
- They give because they have been asked.
- They give to people they respect and trust.
- They give to success—not distress.
- They give to meet the needs of those you serve—not to your needs.
- They give to make the world a better place.

Most people's concept of fundraising is the "tin cup theory." When I was a boy growing up in New Jersey, my mom took me and my brothers and sister to the Radio City Music Hall Christmas Show with the famous Rockettes. We always took a bus into New York City and arrived at the Port Authority bus terminal.

There was always an older man with one leg holding up a tin cup with pencils in front of the terminal begging for money. Thus, my early perception of fundraising was begging for your needs, hence the "tin cup theory." Many nonprofit organizations today still practice and promote the concept of asking for money based on their needs.

Your organizational needs for new facilities, program support, etc., are important, but that is not an effective way to go about it. Your fundraising efforts will become more successful when you begin to frame your fundraising discussions on investing in your success.

Based on the researched principles of philanthropy described above, people give to success, not to distress. Those organizations that have transitioned from the "tin cup" to the "investment theory" have far more success in raising money. Their board members are more comfortable and less fearful of rejection when they ask people to invest in the nonprofit's success, in its positive achievements and results, to documented outcomes, and how the nonprofit makes a difference in the lives of others.

Their board members are more externally focused on what they do for others and not on what the needs of the organization are. Those organizations that develop a culture of philanthropy where everyone understands the principles of philanthropy dramatically increase their level of success in today's fierce competition for the donor dollar.

In all of the thousands of books and articles on fundraising and development, there is one concept that I have rarely heard mentioned, yet it's the key to further engage and motivate your board—the need to increase your board's level of self-confidence.

We have huge unrealistic expectations of our board members related to fundraising. Just because someone is president of the regional bank or vice president of business development for a successful area corporation does not guarantee or translate to success in the world of fundraising and development.

In addition, constantly reminding board members about their role and responsibility as a board member on fundraising is like reminding your kids to clean their room. It rarely is effective (maybe your kids but not mine). When people become confident in their abilities, they generate their own motivation.

Also, during the board recruitment process, the issue of fundraising is rarely brought up by many nonprofit organizations. Yet we expect our boards to know about fundraising and become disappointed when their performance is less than expected. We need to continually educate our board members on why people give money. The more comfortable and knowledgeable your board becomes, the more their level of engagement and activities will increase. In addition to the personal satisfaction and joy that comes from giving, one of the major reasons why people give money, based on the principles of philanthropy, is because someone they know and respect asked them. It is often as simple as that.

Let's now discuss how to avoid "fundraising the Bermuda Triangle."

"Fundraising the Bermuda Triangle" is when all three parties—development officer, chief executive, and board—all point fingers and blame each other for their organization's lack of success. This is based on a lack of solid knowledge and understanding that each role plays (the triangle) in moving the fundraising initiatives forward. Apparently, it is easier to blame others than to own up to their own personal responsibility. It takes a team effort of all three parties.

The average tenure of a development officer is about 18 months. The constant turnover is usually due to the lack of any significant support from either the chief executive officer or members of the board. Far too often, board members ask the chief executive, "How much money has she raised yet? Heck, she's already been on the payroll for over three months!" Common complaints from the development officer are "My CEO won't help me out" or "My board expects me to do it all by myself; they won't make any introductions to their friends for me."

Board members often refuse to feel any responsibility for fundraising when they make statements like "I'll join your board as long as I don't have to raise any money" and they hear "Sure, no problem. We don't expect you to. We have our own development department."

When everyone understands the "tri-partnership of philanthropy" and the role each is expected to perform, the "Bermuda Triangle" can be avoided.

The Role of the Chief Executive Officer:

- Chief sales officer—let people know what you do
- Chief relationship officer—be the face of the organization

- Chief communications officer—let people know your achievements and success
- Chief brand builder—build positive images of your organization
- Chief fundraising officer—be responsible for increasing donors and dollars

The Role of the Board:

- Advocate for your mission.
- Communicate your achievements and outcomes.
- Agree to identify and help cultivate at least three prospective donors, either a family or person, a corporation, or a foundation.
- Be an active participator in special events.
- Write personal notes and letters on annual appeals.
- Make an annual personal contribution based on your means.
- Recognize and thank donors

The Role of the Development Officer:

- Develop a comprehensive and diversified fundraising plan.
- Create a written case for support.
- Quarterback the game plan.
- Build prospect relations.
- Follow through on all initiatives.
- Develop and maintain a donor database.

- Educate the CEO and board.
- Solicit gifts.
- Provide effective stewardship.

When everyone learns that development is a team effort, not a solo practice, the organization will avoid the Bermuda Triangle and achieve greater levels of success. Each party understands their own role and what is expected of them and what they can expect of others. When the organization avoids the Bermuda Triangle, they are becoming an organization that is in *Strategic Alignment*.

Since we now know that people give to success, not distress, make sure every board member, chief executive, and development officer can answer these:

Discussion Questions

- *What is the value we provide to our community?*
- *What are our top achievements and results from this past year?*
- *What is the return on investments that our donors provide us with?*
- *Why are we worthy of someone's gift?*

Chapter 13:
Good Boards Evaluate the CEO; Great Boards Evaluate Themselves

"Without proper self-evaluation, failure is inevitable."

John Wooden

Measuring the Board's Annual Performance

One of the more overlooked responsibilities of a nonprofit board is the requirement to assess its own performance. Most nonprofit boards are familiar with their main responsibilities, such as hiring the CEO, conducting his/her annual evaluation, developing strategic plans, and ensuring the organization has the necessary resources to carry out its mission.

However, they often forget to evaluate how well the responsibilities of the board are being carried out as well as how each member of the board feels about their level of engagement and motivation.

There are two credible options for your board to assess its own performance. One option is to ask board members to complete a board assessment questionnaire that asks a series of questions about the work of the board with a scaled response, such as 1 (lowest or strongly disagree) to 5 (highest or strongly agree). Questions call for a numerical response on a wide range of issues dealing with the organization's mission, programs and services, financial resources, fiscal oversight, CEO performance, board and CEO relationships, board meetings, etc. A summary is prepared after all the responses have been obtained. The relative numerical score indicates areas of strength as well as areas of potential need for improvement.

The advantage of this approach is the ease of execution and timeliness of the reports. On the other hand, questionnaires don't easily allow for open-ended questions that get to "the heart of the matter" for improving the work of the board.

Another option is to engage a professional facilitator who is knowledgeable about nonprofit board governance best practices to perform an assessment. This would include confidential interviews with all members of your board. Open-ended questions and the resulting conversations will help to measure your board members' engagement, how fulfilling and meaningful their experience as a board member has been, and what, if any, recommendations they may have to remove obstacles and improve the work of the board.

From my experience, the most effective way to assess a nonprofit board's performance is to use both strategies—a questionnaire as well as engagement of a trained board facilitator who can ask important open-ended questions that will also measure the level of engagement and motivation of your board members. This approach can be done every few years to augment an annual questionnaire.

Discussion Questions:

- *Does your board perform an annual assessment of its performance?*
- *Does your current assessment process ask open-ended questions?*
- *Would you be interested in measuring your board's level of engagement and motivation?*

- *What are your board's greatest strengths? What are its most important areas of needed improvement?*

Conclusion

I hope you have enjoyed this book. I have enjoyed being here for you. We have covered a lot of important topics in our short time together:

- The stages/life cycles of boards
- Characteristics and obstacles of high-performing boards
- The roles, responsibilities, and characteristics of high-performing board chairs
- The challenges and recommendations related to board leadership succession
- The board and CEO relationship
- Board meetings and agendas
- The annual CEO performance evaluation
- The board's role in achieving your strategic vision
- How to engage your board to actively participate in philanthropy
- Transitioning from the "tin cup" to the "investment" theory of fundraising
- Board committee structures
- Board recruitment best practices and reappointment criteria
- Challenges of dealing effectively with difficult board behaviors
- And, finally, addressing the board's annual performance assessment

I applaud you for your tireless dedication and commitment to your organization's mission and quest for excellence. It is my hope and intention that the information from this book will enable you and your fellow board members to assess your own strengths and decide what, if any, priorities you have for improving your work to become a high-performing nonprofit board. In addition to your own personal satisfaction, the ultimate beneficiaries will be those you serve. I wish you continued success and happiness in your journey.

Dennis C. Miller, Founder & Chairman of DCM Associates, www.dcm-associates.com, is an expert in nonprofit board and leadership coaching and keynotes several motivational speaker events every year. He has turned his 39 years of executive leadership experience into one of the country's most successful nonprofit leadership search firms. His Institute for Nonprofit Board & Executive Leadership provides numerous tools, online courses, assessments, evaluations, surveys, and consultation to help nonprofit organizations grow into their full potential. Dennis can be contacted at dennis@dcm-associates.com.

www.ingramcontent.com/pod-product-compliance
Lightning Source LLC
Chambersburg PA
CBHW031538210526
45464CB00003B/1069